simply jewelry

Designs from the editor of
Stringing magazine

Danielle
Fox

INTERWEAVE PRESS.
interweavebooks.com

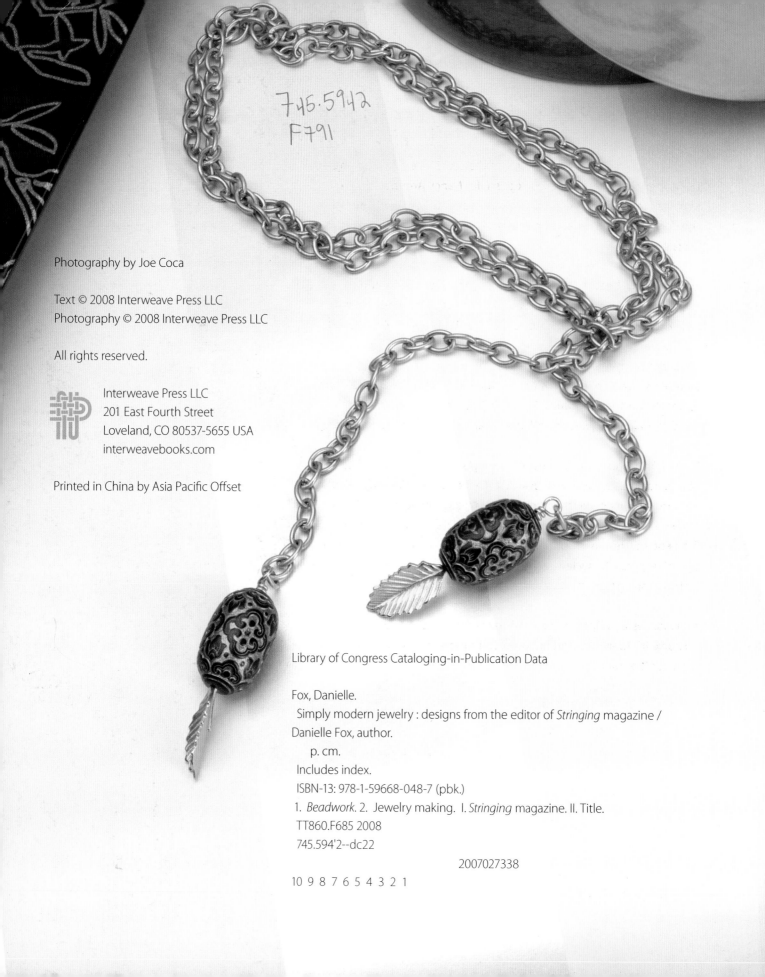

Photography by Joe Coca

Interweave Press LLC
201 East Fourth Street
Loveland, CO 80537-5655 USA
interweavebooks.com

Printed in China by Asia Pacific Offset

Library of Congress Cataloging-in-Publication Data

Fox, Danielle.
 Simply modern jewelry : designs from the editor of *Stringing* magazine /
Danielle Fox, author.
     p. cm.
 Includes index.
 ISBN-13: 978-1-59668-048-7 (pbk.)
 1. *Beadwork*. 2. Jewelry making. I. *Stringing* magazine. II. Title.
 TT860.F685 2008
 745.594'2--dc22

                              2007027338

10 9 8 7 6 5 4 3 2 1

Thanks to the talented editors, designers, and photographers who helped make this book possible: Nancy Arndt, Melinda Barta, Marlene Blessing, Bonnie Brooks, Lisette Bushong, Rebecca Campbell, Joe Coca, Paulette Livers, Connie Poole, Ann Swanson, Katrina Vogel, and Tricia Waddell.

To the friendly beadmakers and vendors who made, found, and/or shipped beading supplies to me, sometimes with very short notice: Jane Acuna, Lisa and Tony Blackwell, Lindsay Burke, Kathy Dannerbeck, Jess Italia-Lincoln, Melanie Brooks Lukacs, Larry and Maude Lorah, Kate McKinnon, Amy Merritt, Sarah Moran, Melissa Nichols, Greg Ogden, Linda Podkova, Renée Renoir, Yvette Rodriguez, Stephanie Sersich, Pam Springall, Jen Thoits, Andrew Thornton, Cynthia Thornton, Katie Wall, Candice Wakumoto, Rebecca Whittaker, and Heather and Pam Wynn.

To my family and friends, whose love, support, and sense of humor have made the last busy year bearable: My boyfriend, Nicolai Ramler, for uncomplainingly putting up with my all-consuming book schedule. My brother, Josh, for offering to help with the book. My sister, Heather, for being my design consultant. My brother-in-law, Tom, for his "encouraging" response to my jewelry: "I would never wear that." And my cousin Holly, for being the president of my fan club.

And most especially to my parents who I know are proud of me, book or no book. It's their unconditional love and support that has dared me to reach for the stars. I love you.

Danielle

contents

I remember the first time I bought a piece of "grown-up" jewelry. It was a necklace of blue-stone links that had a forward-facing clasp decorated with blue-stone dangles. I remember this purchase so well because 1.) I bought it to wear to a dear friend's bridal shower, and 2.) I felt so extravagant spending forty dollars on an accessory. (Mind you, at the time I was a new grad living in Big City Chicago on assistant-to-the-assistant's assistant wages!) I still like the necklace—at least it was a tasteful splurge—but today I have only one thought when I wear it: *I could have made this myself!*

You see, once you learn the fundamental techniques for creating jewelry, you'll realize how easy it is to make the stylish necklaces, bracelets, and earrings you drool over at boutiques and department stores. Really!

I learned how to make simple beaded jewelry on the job. I'm the editor of Interweave Press's *Stringing* magazine, which means that I have had the good fortune of being taught and inspired by talented bead and beaded-jewelry artists.

With this book I hope to pass on to you what I've learned. I'll start by introducing you to the tools, techniques, and supplies you'll need to make your own jewelry. Then with each chapter I'll share a suggestion for how to approach a jewelry project, such as Mix it Up, Play with Symmetry, and Experiment with Sizing, followed by designs that exemplify that chapter's topic. Of course, every project comes with thorough step-by-step instructions and photos.

My wish is that you will find at least one project in this book that you will be dying to make. And when you wear it, you'll be proud to say, *Why, yes, I **did** make this myself!*

shopping for beads & supplies

Shopping for beads and other supplies is half the fun of making jewelry! What follows is a handy guide to the products used in this book. Note that I'm only skimming the surface of what's available. You'll soon discover, if you haven't already, that there's a whole wide world of beading materials out there just waiting for you to play with.

BEADS

A wide variety of beads—or small objects with holes in them—are available today. Explained here are the types of beads most commonly found at bead shops.

Glass

Glass is a versatile medium for beads that can be melted, molded, and combined with other materials for fantastic results.

Seed beads: Tiny glass beads available in endless colors and finishes. Most are produced in Japan or the Czech Republic. Seed bead sizes, which are indicated by the degree symbol (°), vary by producer, but generally range from size 20° to 6° (the smaller the number, the larger the bead). I used sizes 11° and 15° Czech seed beads for the projects in this book.

Lampworked: Handmade beads created by working hot glass rods over a flame (in the old days, a lamp; today, a propane torch).

Fire-polished: Glass beads (generally from the Czech Republic) that are faceted to catch light and often have a surface finish applied to them for extra sparkle. Fire-polished beads resemble crystals and, being less expensive, are often used in their place.

Pressed-glass: Glass beads (generally from the Czech Republic) that are made by pressing glass into molds. They come in a variety of colors and shapes, including rounds, daggers, flowers, leaves, and more.

Clay

A material that is malleable while moist but becomes hard when fired. Types of clay include porcelain, ceramic, stoneware, and earthenware.

Polymer clay: Beads made from a claylike plastic that can be baked in an oven rather than being fired in a kiln.

Raku: Glazed ceramic beads made out of earthenware clay that is fired at a high temperature using a technique that yields a beautiful metallic, crackled, and/or variegated finish.

Crystal

Leaded glass beads that, more often than not, are produced by the Austrian company Swarovski. Crystals come in various sizes, shapes, colors, and finishes.

Cubic Zirconia (CZ)

Beads made from synthetic zirconium oxide, a mineral that closely resembles diamonds both in weight and appearance.

Pearl

A precious commodity causing people throughout the ages to go to tremendous lengths to retrieve it from its watery home. Today there are several alternatives to expensive natural pearls:

Freshwater: Pearls cultured in inland lakes and rivers. These are genuine pearls, though an irritant is manually inserted into an oyster to stimulate their production. Freshwater pearls are offered in innumerable sizes, shapes, and colors.

Crystal: Made by Swarovski, these "pearls" have a crystal core coated with a pearl-like substance. They are perfectly shaped and have a weight similar to that of genuine pearls.

Sequin

A small, usually sparkly, disc-shaped bead.

Plastic

A versatile man-made material used in thousands of products, plastic is also a great option for lightweight beads.

Lucite: A plastic created in the 1930s for use in fighter planes and later used for costume jewelry. Beads made of this material are vibrantly colored and available in countless shapes, sizes, and colors.

Resin: Though resin is a liquid produced by plants, resin beads are actually made of synthetic resin—in other words, plastic. They are durable, translucent, and available in many candylike colors.

Semiprecious Stone

Natural, nonprecious stone beads such as turquoise, aquamarine, opal, apetite, and citrine. Semi-precious stones are valuable but are not as rare or as expensive as precious stones.

Charm

Tiny (often metal) pendants used in charm bracelets, on necklaces, or as embellishments for jewelry.

Vintage

Beads that are old (but may not appear so) and usually collector's items. Often vintage molds are purchased by contemporary companies so that vintage designs can be produced again.

BEAD SHAPES vary greatly. Here are some of the most common bead shapes. It is fun to experiment with a variety of shapes in your designs.

barrel | bicone | chiclet | chips | cube | keishi
oval | potato | rice | rondelle | round | teardrops

BEAD SIZES are measured in millimeters, except for seed beads, which have their own sizing system (see seed bead sizes, right). Bead measurements are given as width by height.

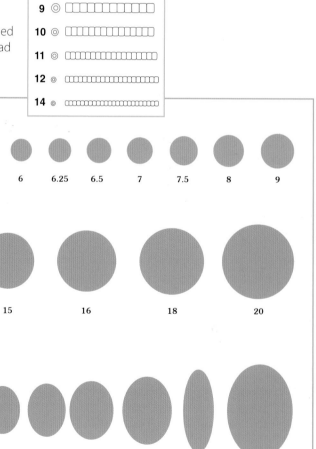

7 ◎
8 ◎
9 ◎
10 ◎
11 ◎
12 ◎
14 ◎

Round

2   2.5   2.75   3   3.5   4   4.5   5   5.5   6   6.25   6.5   7   7.5   8   9

10   11   12   14   15   16   18   20

Oval

3 × 5   5 × 6   5 × 7   6 × 8   7 × 9   8 × 10   9 × 11   10 × 12   10 × 14   12 × 16   13 × 18   8 × 22   18 × 25

JEWELRY MAKING MATERIALS

Almost anything that can be strung through beads or pendants can be used for jewelry making. The following are some materials that are commonly used.

Beading wire: Strong, flexible wire that is made of multiple thin steel wires that have been coated with nylon. The more strands of wires used, the more flexible the beading wire. Use .014 or .015 to string lighter beads or .018 or .019 to string heavier beads.

Metal wire: Used for wireworking, metal wire is available in various gauges and tempers. My favorite gauges (or thicknesses) are 22- and 24-gauge wire (the lower the number, the thicker the wire): 22-gauge is about 0.6mm thick and 24-gauge is about 0.5mm thick. My favorite temper (hardness or softness) is half-hard because it is malleable but will maintain a bend or loop well.

Leather cord: Usually made of cowhide, the best quality leather cord is generally considered to be Greek leather cord.

Memory wire: A hard steel wire that is permanently coiled and comes in sizes for rings, bracelets, and necklaces. Do not use your nice wire/flush cutters with memory wire—it will ruin them! Use special memory-wire cutters instead.

Ribbon: A narrow strip of fabric, often silk or satin. Using ribbon is a great way to incorporate a different stringing material or embellishment into your designs.

OTHER COMMONLY USED TERMS AND MATERIALS

Bail: A loop on which a pendant can be suspended.

Bezel: An empty cavity with a rim that can be filled with stones, resin, and more.

Pendant: A suspended ornament, usually the focal piece of a necklace.

Spacer: A small bead, often round or rondelle, used between other larger beads to set them apart and draw attention to them.

METALS

Metal is often sold by weight and varies greatly in price. Components made from precious metals, such as gold-filled or sterling silver, are more expensive than those made from base, or nonprecious, metals such as brass or copper.

Brass: An alloy of copper and zinc. Brass is not a precious metal so it is affordable and has a nice antique appeal.

Copper: A reddish metallic element that oxidizes easily. When copper interacts with skin it can leave a green residue that is harmless and easy to wash off.

Fine silver: Silver that is 99.9 percent pure silver. When heated at a high temperature, the stabilizers in Precious Metal Clay (PMC)—a popular material for making beads, pendants, and charms—burn off, leaving behind fine silver.

German metal: Beads that are cast in tin; plated with sterling silver, 22k gold, oxidized silver, and other metals; and are then matted and covered with a lacquer. They are manufactured in Germany.

Gold-filled: Describes when a base metal, such as brass or nickel, is bonded with a layer of gold.

Pewter: A metal alloy of tin with a little copper. Avoid pewter beads that also contain lead. Pewter is a dull silver color and, as such, is often used in place of sterling silver for a less shiny look.

Brass

Copper

Fine silver

German metal

Gold-filled

Pewter

Rhodium: A silvery white metallic element that is related to platinum and is the most expensive precious metal. It does not oxidize, and is often plated on other metals.

Shibuichi: An alloy of silver and copper that when heated produces beautiful pink, green, blue, yellow, and purple colors.

Sterling silver: An alloy of silver and copper. To be sold legally as sterling silver, beads must be 92.5 percent silver (the other 7.5 percent is copper) and marked as such (this is the 925 stamp that you see on sterling silver).

Thai silver: The type of silver made by the Karen hill tribe people in Thailand. They use old car parts and other found objects as tools to make their beads. Thai silver is typically 95 to 99 percent pure silver.

Vermeil: Sterling silver beads coated with at least 10k gold.

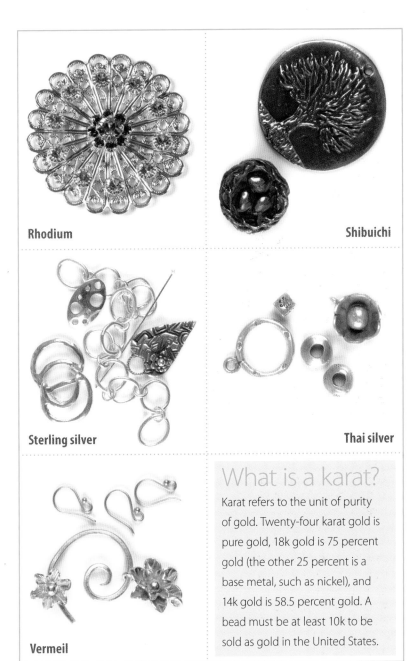

Rhodium

Shibuichi

Sterling silver

Thai silver

Vermeil

What is a karat?

Karat refers to the unit of purity of gold. Twenty-four karat gold is pure gold, 18k gold is 75 percent gold (the other 25 percent is a base metal, such as nickel), and 14k gold is 58.5 percent gold. A bead must be at least 10k to be sold as gold in the United States.

tools & techniques

Luckily, you don't need to use many tools or techniques to make fabulous jewelry. In fact, the projects featured in this book were created using only five tools and five techniques.

Tools
When purchasing your tools, opt for the best quality you can afford; they work better and last longer than lower-end tools.

Wire or flush cutters have sharp edges that cut beading wire and gauged wire straight and evenly. **Do not,** however, use wire or flush cutters with memory wire, a very hard steel wire used in the project on page 112; the wire will ruin your tool. Instead use *memory-wire cutters*.

Flat- and chain-nose pliers have smooth jaws that are used to grip and create bends in metal wire. The jaws of chain-nose pliers are more tapered than those of flat-nose pliers, so the former are better at reaching into small spaces while the latter are better at gripping wider surfaces. Either will work for the projects in this book, though I only list flat-nose pliers in the tools lists. Having one of each is the best scenario.

Round-nose pliers have smooth, conical jaws that are used to make loops with metal wire.

Crimping pliers mold a 2x2mm or 2x1mm crimp tube around beading wire to provide a secure finish to a project.

Scissors are needed for cutting silk and leather.

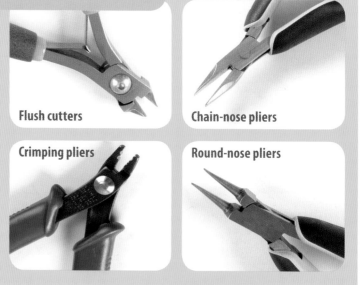

Flush cutters

Chain-nose pliers

Crimping pliers

Round-nose pliers

Accessories
Here are a few more items you may want to have in your workspace.

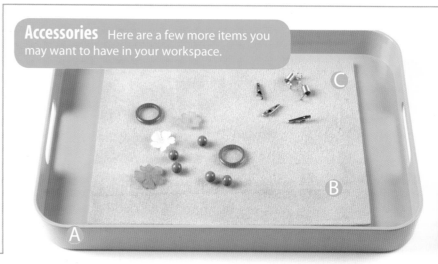

A. BEAD TRAY
Contain your projects (and spills!) in a tray. While you can certainly buy fancy bead-specific trays or bead boards, I'm pretty happy with my plastic Target-bought serving tray!

B. BEADING BLANKET
Your beads won't go anywhere if you work with them on a piece of Vellux cloth (think nylon hotel blanket). Buy them at beading stores or cut up a blanket.

C. ALLIGATOR CLIPS and BEAD STOPS
These handy tools clip or cinch onto the ends of beading wire to prevent beads from falling off already-strung strands.

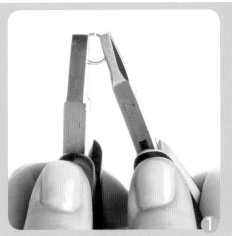
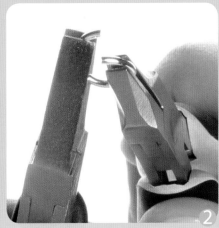

Opening and closing jump rings is not a difficult task, but it takes more skill than you might imagine.

1: Grasp each side of the opening of a jump ring with pliers (preferably two flat-nose pliers; round-nose pliers usually mar the metal).

2: Twist the sides of the jump ring in opposite directions, one side straight toward you and one side straight away from you. Do not pull them apart.

3: String whatever you want to attach to the jump ring, then twist the sides of the jump ring in opposite directions again to close.

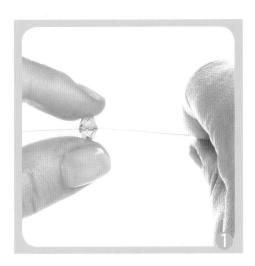

Stringing is the easiest of the techniques. It means putting beads onto wire or silk or whatever material you're using to hold your beads.

1: Thread the beading wire (or whatever stringing material you're using) through the bead's hole.

techniques

Crimping is only slightly more complicated than stringing. It is a two-part technique by which you mold a crimp tube around beading wire using crimping pliers. Most often this technique is used to attach a clasp to a piece of jewelry, thereby creating a secure finish; sometimes, however, the technique is used to "float" beads on wire (see the project on page 62). The instructions that follow are for attaching a clasp.

1: String a crimp tube onto your beading wire.

2: String one half of the clasp, then pass back through the crimp tube, leaving a short tail.

3: Slide the tube toward the clasp, making sure it's snug, yet loose enough to allow the loop to move freely on the clasp. Hold the two wires in your crimp tube so that they are not crossing over each other.

4: Use the back notch of the crimping pliers to press the tube down over the wires. Each wire should now be contained in its own chamber.

5: Rotate the crimp tube forty-five degrees before gripping it in the front notch of the pliers. Squeeze the pliers to fold the two chambers onto themselves, forming a tight cylinder.

6: Trim excess wire.

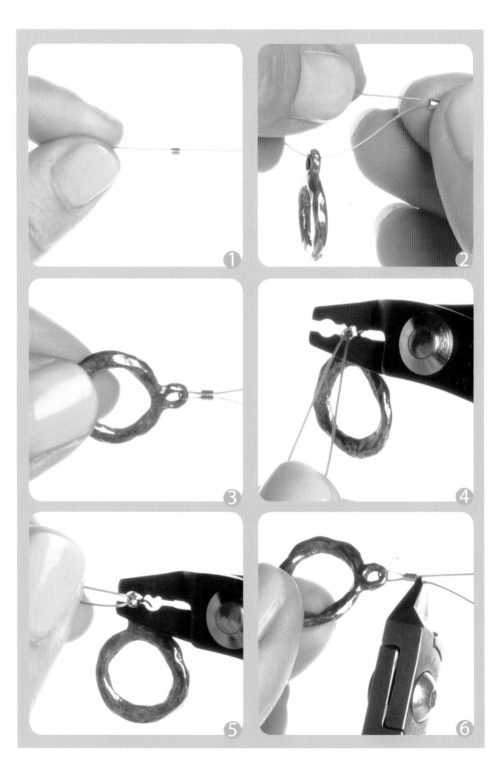

etc. . . .

It is important to note here that the crimp tubes are different than crimp beads. Crimp tubes are cylindrical and are meant to be used with crimping pliers. Crimp beads are round and are meant to be flattened with flat-nose pliers. I prefer using crimp tubes as I feel they are more secure than crimp beads.

Placing a crimp cover over a crimp tube hides unattractive tubes:

1: Gently press the crimp tube into the mouth of a crimp cover. I like to make sure the seam of the crimp cover will be on the underside of the piece.

2: Grasp the crimp cover with the front notch of the crimping pliers and gently squeeze the cover closed. If necessary, rotate the crimp cover in the front notch of the crimping pliers and gently squeeze at intervals to form a uniformly round crimp cover.

3: When you are all done you should have what looks like a round silver bead.

techniques

Wireworking takes practice, but once you get the hang of it, you can take your jewelry making to the next level. The steps for performing the most common wireworking techniques are described below.

Creating a Simple Loop:

A simple loop is the preferred loop for creating a dangle or link with a bead that is not heavy. To form a simple loop (here on a head pin), do the following:

1: String a bead or beads on a head pin. Use flat-nose pliers to make a ninety-degree bend at the top of the bead.

2: Imagine the size of the loop you would like to make, then place the nose of the round-nose pliers on the bent wire at a distance from the fold that equals about half the circumference of the loop you imagined. Holding the piece of wire with the bent end facing you, roll the pliers away from you, toward the bend, but not past it.

3: Using your fingers, continue the wrap around the nose of the pliers.

4: Trim the wire next to the bend. You can open and close a simple loop as you would a jump ring.

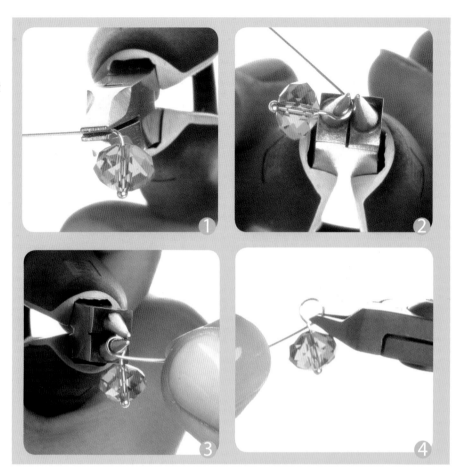

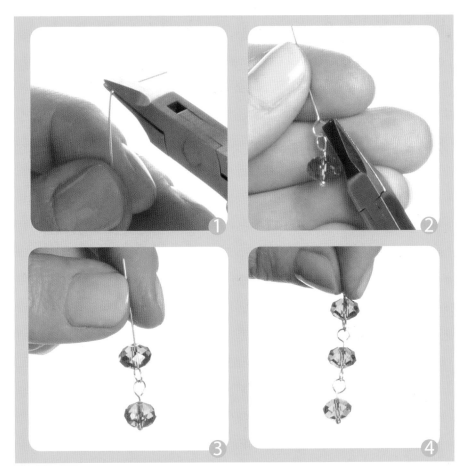

Creating

A simple
wire wit
attachir
etc. To
following:

1: Make a ninety-degree bend ½" (1 cm) from one end of a piece of wire.

2: Form a simple loop that attaches to whatever you want to link it to.

3: Trim the wire next to the bend, then string a bead or beads.

4: Make another simple loop on the other side of the bead that attaches to whatever you want to link it to. Trim the wire next to the bead.

...ting a Wrapped Loop:

A wrapped loop is a sturdy loop that's preferable when creating a dangle that is heavy or will incur strain. To form a wrapped loop (here on a head pin), do the following:

1: String a bead or beads on a head pin. Use flat-nose pliers to make a ninety-degree bend about $1/16$–$1/8$" (2–4mm) from the top of the bead.

2: Imagine the size of the loop you would like to make, then place the nose of the round-nose pliers on the bent wire at a distance from the fold that equals about half the circumference of the loop you imagined. Holding the piece of wire with the bent end facing you, roll the pliers away from you, toward the bend, but not past it.

3: Hold the loop with flat-nose pliers. Use your fingers or another pair of pliers to wrap the tail wire down the neck of the main wire to the top of the bead (about two or three coils). Trim the wire next to the bead.

4: Once you've trimmed the wire after making coils, press the end down with either flat-nose pliers or the front notch of crimping pliers so it doesn't stick out.

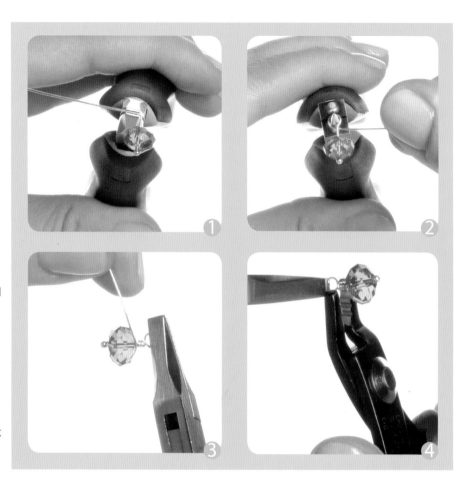

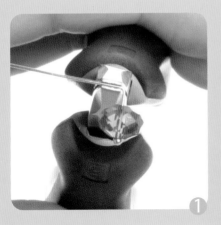

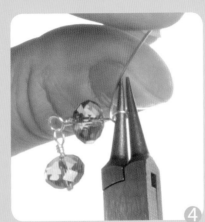

Note: In images 3 and 5, I'm using round-nose pliers to hold the wire because space is tight. Be aware that these might mar the wire. Use chain-nose pliers instead whenever possible.

Creating a Wrapped-Loop Link:

A wrapped-loop link is a bead with wrapped loops on each end for attaching to other loops, chains, clasps, etc. To form a wrapped-loop link, do the following:

1: Use flat-nose pliers to make a ninety-degree bend 2" (5 cm) from one end of a piece of wire.

2: Use round-nose pliers to form a loop that attaches to whatever you want to link it to.

3: Wrap the tail wire down the neck of the main wire (about two or three coils).

4: Trim the wire, then string a bead or beads.

5: Make another wrapped loop on the other end of the bead that attaches to whatever you want to link it to. Trim the wire next to the bead.

find your

inspiration

I don't think it's possible for one person to tell another how to be inspired to make a piece of jewelry. But I do think it's possible to help someone recognize inspiration when they see it.

Have you ever lingered over a picture of Nicole Kidman in *People* magazine because she was wearing an incredible pair of earrings? You've been inspired by the style of her earrings. Do you want a necklace to go with a special dress you just bought? That dress is your inspiration. Have you ever saved a piece of wrapping paper because it was so pretty, you couldn't stand to throw it away? The wrapping paper: your inspiration.

Translating inspiration into beautiful, wearable pieces of jewelry is the subject of this chapter. Following are examples that show how inspiration—in the form of clothes, pictures from magazines, trends, occasions, and more—guided the direction of my jewelry designs.

Golden Everglades

inspired by attire

I recently purchased a beautiful silk dress in soft shades of green. To be honest, I'll probably end up admiring it more than wearing it—it's a little too dressy for work and not quite dressy enough for a night out.

Still, I was compelled to design something to wear with my fabulous find. I thought a long necklace would suit its V-neckline. And since it was the unusual mix of colors that attracted me to the dress, I picked out some Swarovski crystals in shades to match. For chain and components, I went with gold vermeil—the greens of the dress and crystals really sing next to the warm gold. Perhaps some day I'll be invited to a garden party I can wear the ensemble to!

MATERIALS

4 apple green opaque 8mm vintage crystal rounds

4 light azore champagne 8mm crystal rounds

4 jet 8mm crystal rounds

4 jonquil matte 8mm crystal rounds

4 emerald 8mm crystal rounds

6 vermeil 20mm ring links

6 gold-filled 8mm jump rings

1 vermeil 25mm hook-and-eye clasp

18" (45.5 cm) of vermeil 7x17mm rectangular chain

60" (152.5 cm) of gold-filled 22-gauge half-hard wire

TOOLS

Wire cutters

Flat-nose pliers

Round-nose pliers

FINISHED SIZE

35" (89 cm)

TECHNIQUES

Wireworking; opening and closing jump rings

SIMPLICITY SCALE

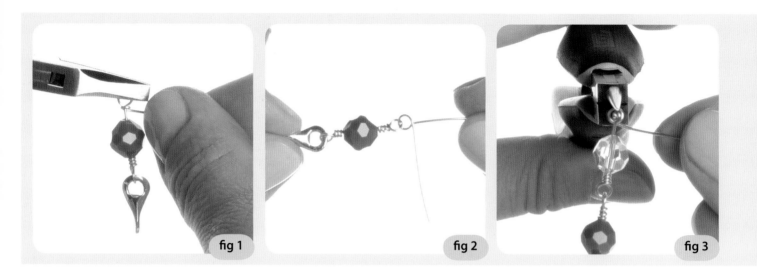

fig 1

fig 2

fig 3

etc....

Some of the crystals I used may be hard to find: apple green because it is vintage and light azore champagne and jonquil matte because they have special finishes. If you can't find them, either substitute with other colors and/or finishes or search the Internet—many bead shops and websites sell crystals (see Resources, pages 118–119).

1: Cut the wire into twenty 3" (7.5 cm) pieces. Cut the chain into two 8-link (4½" or 11.5 cm) pieces and one 12-link (6½" or 16.5 cm) piece.

2: Use 1 wire to form a wrapped loop that attaches to one half of the clasp. String 1 apple green crystal, then form a wrapped loop **(figure 1)**.

3: Use 1 wire to form a wrapped loop that attaches to the previous wrapped loop **(figure 2)**. String 1 light azore champagne crystal, then form a wrapped loop **(figure 3)**.

4: Repeat Step 3 twice, first with 1 jet crystal, then with 1 jonquil matte crystal.

5: Use 1 wire to form a wrapped loop that attaches to the previous wrapped loop. String 1 emerald crystal, then form a wrapped loop that attaches to 1 ring link **(figure 4)**.

6: Use 1 jump ring to attach the ring link just used to one end of one 8-link (4½" or 11.5 cm) piece of chain **(figure 5)**. Use 1 jump ring to attach the other end of the chain to another ring link.

7: Repeat Step 2, this time attaching the first wrapped loop to the ring link just used, instead of the clasp. Repeat Steps 3–5. Set this half of the necklace aside.

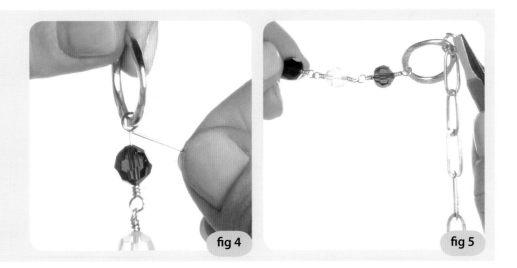

fig 4

fig 5

8: Repeat Step 2 with the other half of the clasp. Repeat Steps 3–7.

9: Use 1 jump ring to attach one end of the 12-link (6½" or 16.5 cm) piece of chain to the last ring link of one half of the necklace. Use 1 jump ring to attach the other end of the chain to the last ring link of the other half of the necklace.

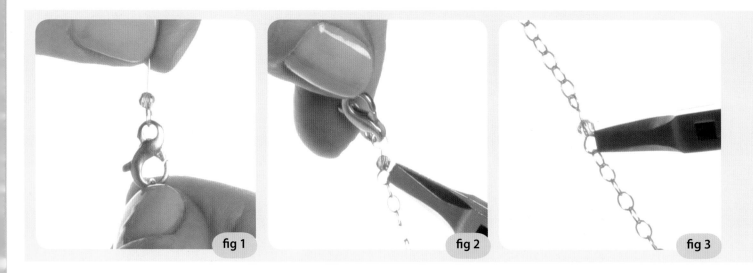

fig 1 fig 2 fig 3

1: Cut the chain into one 26-link (2½" or 6.5 cm) piece and eight 12-link (1¼" or 3 cm) pieces. Cut the 24-gauge wire into ten 1" (2.5 cm) pieces.

2: Use 1 wire to form a simple loop that attaches to the clasp **(figure 1)**. String 1 amethyst crystal and form a simple loop that attaches to one end of one 12-link (1¼" or 3 cm) piece of chain **(figure 2)**.

3: Use 1 wire to form a simple loop that attaches to the other end of the chain just used. String 1 light amethyst crystal and form a simple loop that attaches to one end of another 12-link (1¼" or 3 cm) piece of chain **(figure 3)**.

4: Use 1 wire to form a simple loop that attaches to the other end of the chain just used. String 1 amethyst crystal and form a simple loop that attaches to one end of another 12-link (1¼" or 3 cm) piece of chain.

5: Repeat Step 3.

fig 4

6: Use 1 wire to form a simple loop that attaches to the other end of the chain just used. String 1 amethyst crystal and form a simple loop that attaches to one end of the 26-link (2½" or 6.5 cm) piece of chain. String the pendant over the chain **(figure 4)**.

7: Repeat Step 4. Repeat Step 3. Repeat Step 4. Repeat Step 3.

8: Use the last wire to form a simple loop that attaches to the other end of the chain just used. String 1 light amethyst crystal and form a simple loop that will serve as the other half of the clasp.

etc....

This necklace looks nice when the loops of the crystal links are the same size as the chain links (about 2mm). To get consistent loops, use a piece of tape to mark where on the round-nose pliers to make your loops.

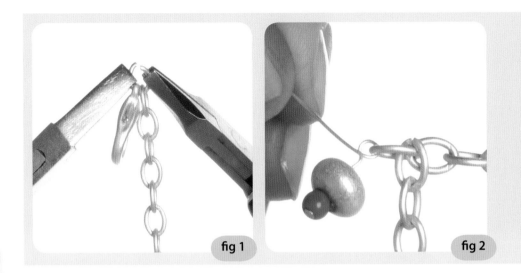

fig 1

fig 2

1: Open the first link of chain, string the clasp, then close the link **(figure 1)**. *This particular chain has unsoldered (severed) links, so instead of cutting it, you can open the links like jump rings to adjust the chain.*

2: Use a head pin to string 1 wasabi round and 1 silver rondelle. Form a wrapped loop that attaches to the fourth link from one end of the chain **(figure 2)**. Repeat to add 1 silver dangle to each of the next 23 links.

etc....

This bracelet is heavy! To support the beads, I made sure the chain and the clasp I used were strong and sturdy.

fig 3

Glass Rules!

Lampworked glass beads are so much fun to look at because they are like colorful little works of art encapsulated in small spheres of glass. And, lucky for us, it seems that most lampworked bead artists create sets of small rondelle beads, which are fun to incorporate into jewelry designs for a nice splash of color. With so many to choose from, the possibilities are endless!

3: Use a head pin to string 1 wasabi round and 1 lampworked rondelle. Form a wrapped loop that attaches to the fifth link of the chain (**figure 3**). You will now have 1 silver dangle and 1 lampworked dangle attached to the same link. Repeat with the remaining head pins and lampworked rondelles to add 1 lampworked dangle to every other link.

4: Adjust the chain to your desired length by removing extra links, if necessary.

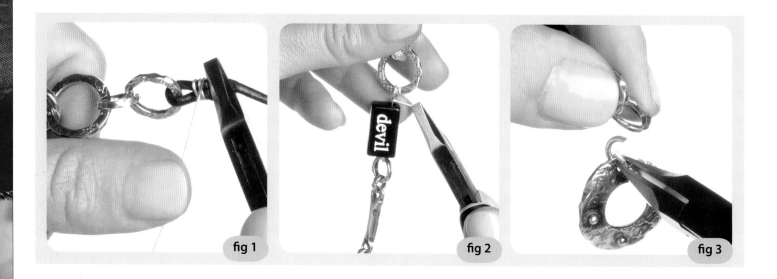

fig 1   fig 2   fig 3

1: Divide the chain into two sets of three pieces. Each piece in the set should be a different length to add interest, but the total length of the three pieces in each set should equal 5½" (14 cm).

2: String one end of one piece of chain on the leather. Form a loop around the chain by bending the end ½" (1.5 cm) of leather over the chain link, then wrap it in place with 5" (12.5 cm) of wire (**figure 1**).

3: Use 3" (7.5 cm) of wire to form a wrapped loop that attaches to the other end of the piece of chain just used. String the "angel" or "devil" bead, then form a wrapped loop that attaches to one end of another piece of chain (**figure 2**).

4: Use 2½" (6.5 cm) of wire to form a wrapped loop that attaches to the other end of the chain just used. String 1 black pressed-glass rectangle, then form a wrapped loop that attaches to one end of another piece of chain. Use 1 jump ring to attach the other end of the chain to one half of the clasp (**figure 3**).

5: Repeat Steps 2–4 for the other half of the necklace.

etc....

These fine silver components were handmade from PMC (Precious Metal Clay) by a talented artist. For a more economical necklace, use store-bought sterling silver or silver-plated chain.

43

Snap Fizz Pop

MATERIALS

5 bottle-blue 8mm pressed-glass rondelles

6 assorted 22mm soda bottle cap beads

12 Thai silver 7mm snowflake spacers

1 sterling silver 22mm toggle clasp

2 sterling silver 2mm crimp tubes

2 sterling silver 3mm crimp covers

9" (23 cm) of silver-plated .018 beading wire

TOOLS

Wire cutters

Crimping pliers

FINISHED SIZE

7¼" (18.5 cm)

TECHNIQUES

Stringing; crimping

SIMPLICITY SCALE

Snap Fizz Pop
try new beads

It's always fun to see the kinds of things people have turned into beads: vintage tins, magazine pages, dice, typewriter keys, and now even bottle caps.

When I saw these novel bottle cap beads by Cathy Collison, I was compelled to test them out. What I came up with is a bracelet that plays out the whole soda bottle theme: cap beads separated by glass bottle blue rondelles and finished with a bubbly-print sterling silver clasp. Are you thirsty yet?

1: Use the beading wire to string 1 crimp tube and one half of the clasp. Pass back through the tube and crimp. Trim excess wire, then cover the tube with a crimp cover.

2: String 1 snowflake spacer. String {1 bottle cap bead, 1 snowflake spacer, 1 blue rondelle, and 1 snowflake spacer} five times. String 1 bottle cap bead, 1 snowflake spacer, 1 crimp tube, and the other half of the clasp. Pass back through the tube and crimp. Trim excess wire, then cover the tube with a crimp cover (**figure 1**).

etc....

Have your own special bottle caps? Send them to Cathy, and she'll make them into beads for you! (See Resources on pages 118–119 for more information.)

fig 1

55

Twiggy
mingle metals

This necklace throws matchy-matchy metals to the wind. I was inspired to this carefree philosophy by the twig pendants. One is sterling silver with a brass bail while the other is bronze. To combine them in a necklace would mean opening the doors to mixing metals—something I hadn't tried before.

I used a medley of chains—copper, brass, sterling silver, and vermeil—attached with shibuichi (an alloy of copper and silver that, when heated, yields beautiful colors) connectors and tiny bird beads in different metal finishes. I was surprised at how well the different metals worked together. The finished product is a hodgepodge—but a happy hodgepodge at that. And I think the twigs look quite at home.

MATERIALS

3 turquoise 3x6mm rondelles

3 pewter 10x6mm birdies (1 each in cast antique brass, silver, and copper)

1 sterling silver 9x9mm pine cone charm

1 sterling silver 14x30mm leaf charm

2 metal 68mm twig pendants (1 sterling silver with brass, 1 bronze)

1 vermeil 18mm toggle clasp

3½" (9 cm) of brushed sterling silver 10mm flat round chain

4¾" (12 cm) of brass 7–9mm flat round chain

6" (15 cm) of antique copper 1x2mm oval chain

1¾" (4.5 cm) of vermeil German metal 5x7mm oval chain

1 shibuichi 29mm tree pendant

3 shibuichi 12x32mm "Love Life" leaf links

9 assorted metal 5–8mm jump rings

6" (15 cm) each of the following wires: brown 22-gauge craft wire, 24-gauge sterling silver wire, and 24-gauge gold-filled wire

TOOLS

Wire cutters

Flat-nose pliers

Round-nose pliers

FINISHED SIZE

19" (48.5 cm)

TECHNIQUES

Wireworking; opening and closing jump rings

SIMPLICITY SCALE

Big Sky Bling

MATERIALS

6 blue/brown 8x12mm raku rondelles

2 Thai silver 8mm flower-stamped spacers

2 Thai silver 9mm daisy spacers

4 Thai silver 10x8mm leaf-stamped barrels

3 sterling silver 8–10x7–11mm bumpy barrels

1 sterling silver 18mm button with shank

10" (25.5 cm) of dark brown 2mm Greek leather cord

TOOL

Scissors

FINISHED SIZE

6½" (16.5 cm)

TECHNIQUES

Knotting; stringing

SIMPLICITY SCALE

H

Here, leather teams up with silver barrel beads and earthy raku beads, all common jewelry-making components that never go out of style. The resulting bracelet is a modern take on cowgirl chic.

1: Fold the leather 1¼" (3 cm) from one end. Tie an overhand knot, leaving a loop large enough for the button to fit through (**figure 1**).

2: String one 8mm spacer, 1 Thai silver barrel, 1 raku rondelle, 1 daisy spacer, 1 bumpy barrel, 1 daisy spacer, 1 raku rondelle, 1 Thai silver barrel, 1 raku rondelle, 1 bumpy barrel, 1 raku rondelle, 1 Thai silver barrel, 1 raku rondelle, 1 bumpy barrel, 1 raku rondelle, 1 Thai silver barrel, one 8mm spacer, and the button shank.

3: Fold the end of the leather down to the last bead. Tie an overhand knot and tighten it near the last bead (**figure 2**); trim excess leather.

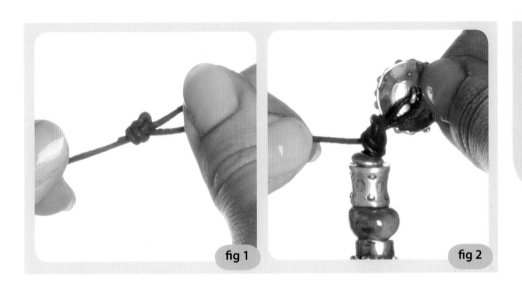

fig 1

fig 2

etc....

Buttons make great clasps! Make a leather loop, as done here, to wrap around the button, or make a loop of seed beads.

Posh Porcupine
leave wire naked

Thanks to beading wire producers, one of the most important jewelry-making materials is now available in finishes you won't always want to hide—a fact I took advantage of when I was designing a necklace that involved floating some unique lampworked "porcupine" beads on wire.

To make this three-strand necklace, I used crimp tubes covered with crimp covers to trap each porcupine bead on its own strand of very pretty, very supple silver-plated wire. And I gave the necklace a casual feel by attaching the beads at different positions on each wire. The result is a piece that is simple, modern, and lightweight.

MATERIALS

3 lampworked porcupine beads (one 20mm, one 23mm, one 26mm)
8 sterling silver 2mm crimp tubes
8 sterling silver 3mm crimp covers
1 sterling silver 21mm slot clasp
46½" (118 cm) of silver-plated .015 beading wire

TOOLS

Wire cutters
Crimping pliers
Pen

FINISHED SIZE

15" (38 cm)

TECHNIQUES

Stringing; crimping

SIMPLICITY SCALE

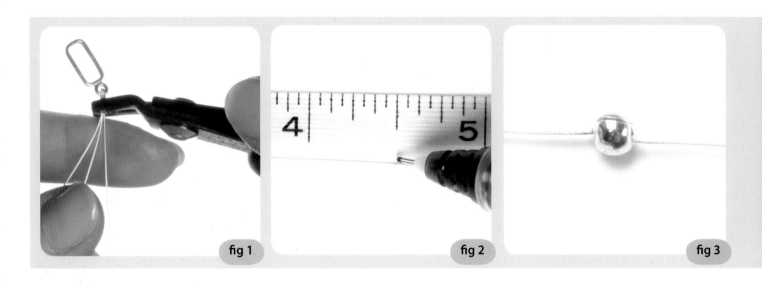

fig 1 fig 2 fig 3

1: Cut the wire into one 16" (40.5 cm) and two 15¼" (38.5 cm) pieces. Line all three wires up at one end with the longest wire to the outside, then use all three wires to string 1 crimp tube and the rectangle half of the clasp. Pass back through the tube and crimp; trim excess wire. Cover the tube with a crimp cover (**figure 1**).

2: Using the short outside wire, measure 4½" (11.5 cm) from the crimp tube and make a small mark with your pen (**figure 2**). String a crimp tube over the mark. Crimp and cover with a crimp cover; do not trim excess wire (**figure 3**).

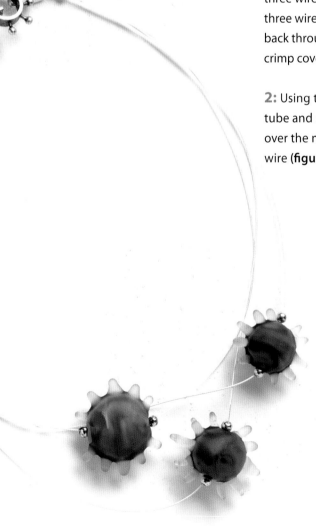

3: String the smallest porcupine bead up to the covered crimp. Make a small mark with the pen on the wire beneath the bead. Unstring the bead, then string a crimp tube over the mark and crimp it (**figure 4**). *Since the bead's hole is big enough to fit over the crimp, I recommend removing the bead before crimping the second crimp tube. Otherwise the little arms on the beads make it difficult to get the crimping pliers close enough to crimp the tube.* Again, do not trim excess wire. Restring the smallest bead up to the covered crimp (**figure 5**). Cover the tube with a crimp cover. The bead should now be trapped on the wire between the two covered crimp tubes.

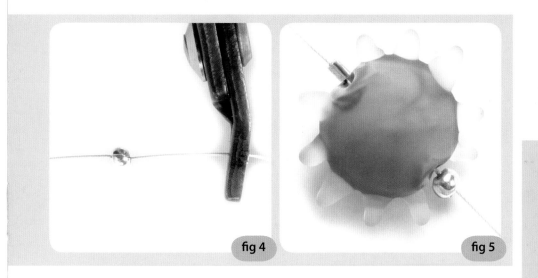

fig 4

fig 5

4: Repeat Step 2, using the middle wire and measuring 5¾" (14.5 cm) from the crimp tube attached in Step 1. Repeat Step 3, using the largest porcupine bead.

5: Repeat Step 2, using the long outside wire and measuring 5½" (14 cm) from the crimp tube attached in Step 1. Repeat Step 3, using the remaining porcupine bead.

6: Use all three wires to string 1 crimp tube and the slot half of the clasp. Pass back through the tube and crimp; trim excess wire. Cover the tube with a crimp cover.

etc....

Proper crimping is essential to this project. Make sure when you crimp a tube that the wire is properly enclosed in one channel of the tube after the first part of the crimping process. Otherwise the tube may come loose.

Exposed!

Not long ago, in the dark ages of jewelry making, only one color of beading wire existed: gray. Today it's available in every color of the rainbow: red, yellow, purple, green, and blue—plus copper, antique brass, sterling silver, gold-plated, and other metallic finishes. Show off these wonderful wires by leaving them bare—in other words, find a way to expose wire in your jewelry!

play with

symmetry

It's easy to get into the habit of making jewelry that is perfectly symmetrical: one half of the piece mirrors the other half. And there's nothing wrong with that. Symmetrical jewelry is pleasing, orderly, expected. But in this chapter I'm going to show you how to shake up your designs a bit, how to create asymmetrical jewelry that is unexpected and anything but orderly, yet pleasing just the same.

Achieving asymmetrical balance takes practice. Asymmetry, or informal balance, is more difficult to achieve than symmetry, or formal balance, because the designer must plan a design more carefully.

The examples that follow illustrate how the placement of the clasp, the use of different beads on each half of the piece, and the sequence of the beads strung can make for interesting asymmetrical jewelry that is balanced. I hope they inspire you to be more courageous in your own designs.

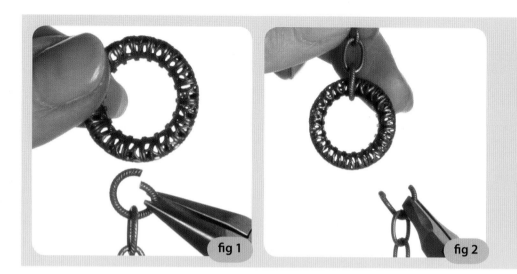

fig 1

fig 2

etc. . . .

These instructions are specific to the chain I used. In other words, I will refer to chain lengths by the number of links, rather than inches. Doing so makes the instructions much easier to describe and follow. If you substitute the chain used here with a chain that has different-size links, adjust the instructions accordingly.

1: Remove two 2-link ($5/8$" or 1.5 cm) pieces and two 3-link ($7/8$" or 2 cm) pieces from the chain. *This particular chain has unsoldered (severed) links, so instead of cutting it, you can open the links like jump rings to adjust the chain.*

2: Use one 9.5mm jump ring to attach one end of one 2-link piece of chain to 1 filigree ring (**figure 1**). Use one 9.5mm jump ring to attach one end of one 3-link piece of chain to the same filigree ring (**figure 2**).

3: Use one 9.5mm jump ring to attach the other end of the 3-link chain just used to 1 filigree ring. Use one 9.5mm jump ring to attach one end of the remaining 3-link piece of chain to the same filigree ring.

4: Use one 9.5mm jump ring to attach the other end of the 3-link chain just used to 1 filigree ring. Use one 9.5mm jump ring to attach one end of the remaining 2-link piece of chain to the same filigree ring.

You should now have a chain with components in the following order: two-link chain (1, 2), filigree ring, 3-link chain (3, 4, 5), filigree ring, 3-link chain (6, 7, 8), filigree ring, and 2-link chain (9, 10). In the steps that follow, I will refer to the chain links by number in the order that they appear here.

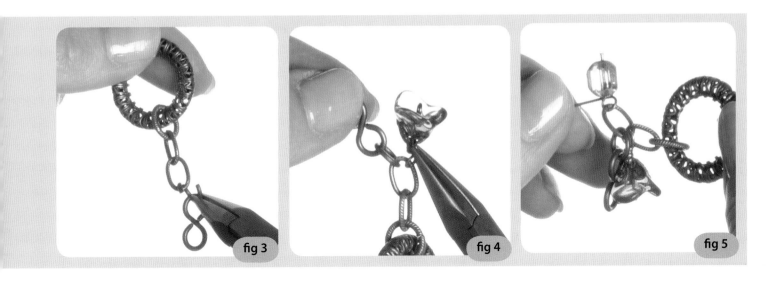

fig 3

fig 4

fig 5

5: Use one 8mm jump ring to attach one half of the clasp to Link 1 (**figure 3**). Repeat to attach the other half of the clasp to Link 10.

6: Use an eye pin to string 1 light green 3-petal flower (wide end first) and one 7.9x5.5mm bead cap and form a wrapped loop that attaches to Link 1 (**figure 4**). Repeat three times to attach a light green 3-petal flower to Links 4, 7, and 10.

7: Use a 2" (5 cm) head pin to string 1 cathedral bead and form a wrapped loop that attaches to Link 1 (**figure 5**). Repeat three times to attach 1 cathedral bead to Links 4, 7, and 10.

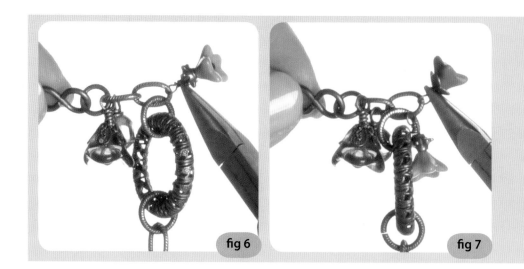

fig 6

fig 7

8: Use a 1½" (3.8 cm) head pin to string 1 turquoise flower (wide end first) and 1 flower spacer; form a wrapped loop that attaches to Link 2 (**figure 6**). Repeat three times to attach 1 turquoise flower to Links 3, 8, and 9.

9: Use a 1½" (3.8 cm) head pin to string 1 olive flower (wide end first) and 1 scalloped or flower bead cap; form a wrapped loop that attaches to Link 2 (**figure 7**). Repeat three times to attach 1 olive flower to Links 5, 6, and 9.

10: Use a one 1½" (3.8 cm) head pin to string 1 yellow flower (wide end first); form a wrapped loop that attaches to Link 4. Repeat to attach 1 yellow flower to Link 7.

fig 8

fig 9

fig 10

11: Use one 4.5mm jump ring to attach 1 filigree teardrop to Link 2 (**figure 8**). Repeat three times to attach 1 filigree teardrop to Links 3, 8, and 9.

12: Use one 4.5mm jump ring to attach the butterfly charm to Link 3 (**figure 9**). Repeat to attach the key charm to Link 4, the heart charm to Link 7, and the dragonfly connector to Link 8.

13: Attach one 4.5mm jump ring to a bird charm, then use another 4.5mm jump ring to attach the jump ring already attached to the bird charm to Link 5 (**figure 10**). Repeat to attach the other bird charm to Link 6.

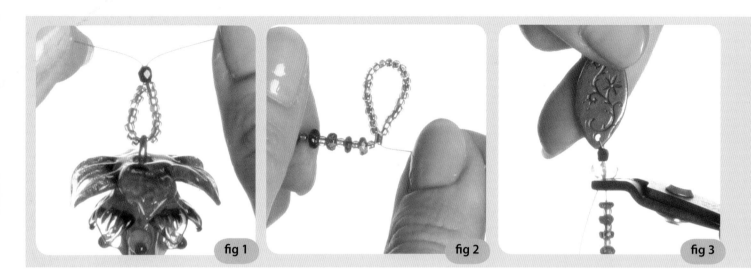

fig 1 fig 2 fig 3

1: String 16 seed beads to the center of the wire. String the lampworked bead over the seed beads. Use both ends of the wire to string 1 fire-polished bead. Snug the fire-polished bead down to the loop, or bail, formed by the seed beads (**figure 1**).

2: Use one wire to string 3 seed beads. On the same wire, string {1 apetite and 1 seed bead} twelve times, omitting the last seed bead. String {1 silver rondelle, 1 citrine, 1 fire-polished bead, and 1 citrine} three times. String 1 silver rondelle. String {1 apetite and 1 seed bead} thirty-five times. String 1 apetite, 1 crimp tube, and 25 seed beads. Pass back through the tube to form a loop (**figure 2**) and crimp; trim excess wire.

etc. . . .

Seed beads are small, but they can have a big impact. Here they form a pretty bail and clasp.

3: Use the other wire to string 3 seed beads. On the same wire, string {1 apetite and 1 seed bead} twelve times, omitting the last seed bead. String 1 crimp tube, 1 citrine, 1 fire-polished bead, and the bottom hole of the "Love" link. Pass back through the fire-polished bead, citrine, and tube. Crimp the tube (**figure 3**) and trim excess wire.

4: Use the remaining wire to string 1 crimp tube, 1 citrine, 1 fire-polished bead and the top hole of the "Love" link. Pass back through the fire-polished bead, citrine, and tube. Crimp the tube (**figure 4**) and trim excess wire. String {1 apetite and 1 seed bead} thirty-five times. String 1 apetite, 1 crimp tube, 10 seed beads, and the bud charm. Pass back through the tube (**figure 5**) and crimp; trim excess wire.

fig 4

fig 5

All Abuzz

MATERIALS

5 black 4x2mm cubic zirconia (CZ) faceted rondelles

6 peach 10–13x12–18mm moonstone nuggets

1 onyx 18x24mm Russian handpainted oval

1 sterling silver 20mm bee box clasp

1 sterling silver 14x10mm bee charm

1 sterling silver 3mm round

1 sterling silver 6mm jump ring

2 sterling silver 2mm crimp tubes

2 sterling silver 3mm crimp covers

10" (25.5 cm) of silver-plated .018 beading wire

TOOLS

Wire cutters

Crimping pliers

FINISHED SIZE

7" (18 cm)

TECHNIQUES

Stringing; crimping

SIMPLICITY SCALE

etc. . . .

Russian handpainted beads are little pieces of art—literally. Each one is signed by the artist.

All Abuzz
concentrate your focal elements

This honey of a bracelet is unusual in the placement of the handpainted onyx focal bead. It's more customary to place the focal bead in the center of the bracelet, instead of buddied up to the clasp. Here's why my arrangement works: Had I centered the focal bead, it would have been overshadowed by the bulk of the box clasp. However, when it's placed next to the clasp, the two work together as one consolidated focal area.

1: Use the wire to string 1 crimp tube and the loop of one half of the clasp. Pass back through the tube and crimp; trim excess wire.

2: String the onyx bead and silver round. String {1 moonstone and 1 CZ} five times. String 1 moonstone, 1 crimp tube, and the loop of the other half of the clasp. Pass back through the tube and crimp (**figure 1**); trim excess wire.

3: Cover the crimp tubes with crimp covers.

4: Use the jump ring to attach the bee charm to one loop of the clasp (**figure 2**).

fig 1

fig 2

81

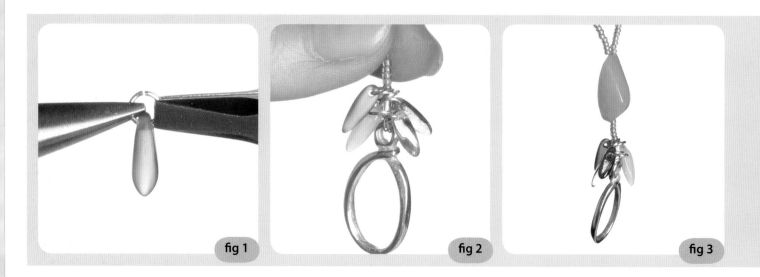

fig 1   fig 2   fig 3

etc. . . .

When choosing lampworked discs for this project, make sure to select ones that have holes large enough to accommodate two strands of seed beads.

1: Attach 1 jump ring to 1 Montana blue dagger (**figure 1**). Repeat to attach 1 jump ring to each dagger.

2: Cut the beading wire in half. Use both wires to string 1 crimp tube and the ring half of the clasp. Pass back through the crimp tube; crimp and trim excess wire.

3: Use both wires to string 6 seed beads and 5 daggers (1 of each color). Slide the jump rings attached to the daggers over the seed beads (**figure 2**). String 1 opal. Use each wire to string 25 seed beads (**figure 3**). Pass one end of the wire through the top and one end through the bottom of the hole of 1 disc. Bring the wires back together on the other side of the disc (**figure 4**). Repeat entire step twice.

4: *Use both wires to string 1 moonstone. String 6 seed beads and 5 daggers (1 of each color). Slide the jump rings attached to the daggers over the seed beads (**figure 5**).* Use each wire to string 25 seed beads. Pass one end of the wire through the top and one end through the bottom of the hole of 1 disc. Bring the wires back together on the other side of the disc. Repeat entire step. Repeat entire step once more from * to *.

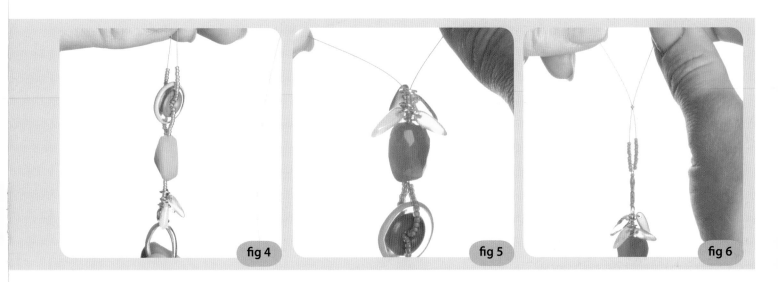

fig 4

fig 5

fig 6

5: Use both wires to string 1 Thai silver tube and 1 seed bead; repeat twice. Use each wire to string 10 seed beads. Use both wires to string 1 seed bead (**figure 6**). Repeat entire step eight times.

6: Use both wires to string 1 crimp tube and the bar (bird) half of the clasp. Pass back through the crimp tube; crimp and trim excess wire.

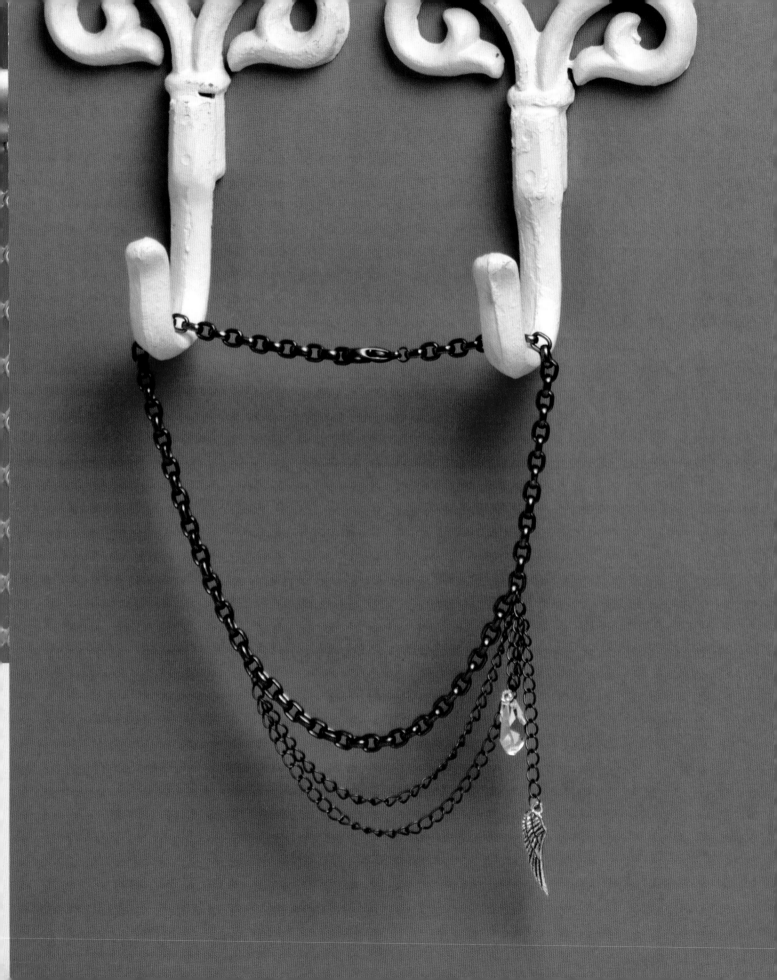

Dark Angel

forget balance

A photograph in a fashion magazine inspired this oxidized-chain necklace. The featured model had donned a long, delicate chain necklace worn loosely knotted around a choker-length chunky chain necklace, its pendant hanging attractively off-center.

I replicated the effect by attaching small-link chain to large-link chain in such a way that the smaller chain forms swags up one side of the necklace. The two pendants—a crystal and an angel wing charm—hang in delicious defiance of symmetry.

I did not even attempt to find balance in this necklace. It is deliberately unsymmetrical, which is refreshing for a change, don't you think?

MATERIALS

1 crystal 17mm polygon drop

1 silver 7x27mm wing charm

5 oxidized German metal 4mm jump rings

13" (33 cm) of oxidized German metal 4x3mm (small) curb chain

15" (38 cm) of oxidized German metal 8x5mm (large) oval chain

1 oxidized German metal 10x18mm lobster clasp

TOOLS

2 pairs of pliers

FINISHED SIZE

16" (40.5 cm)

TECHNIQUE

Opening and closing jump rings

SIMPLICITY SCALE

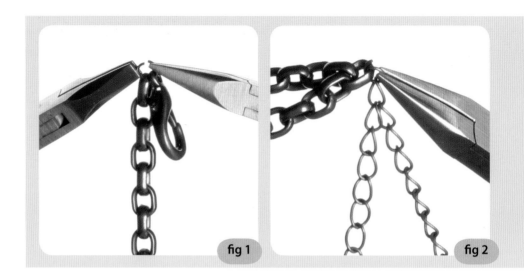

fig 1

fig 2

1: Use 1 jump ring to attach the lobster clasp to one end of the large chain (**figure 1**).

2: Fold the small chain such that one side is 6" (15 cm) long and the other side is 7" (18 cm) long. Use 1 jump ring to attach a link at the fold just created to the large chain 6½" (16.5 cm) from the end without the clasp (**figure 2**).

etc. . . .

Grip the jump rings firmly with flat-nose pliers to attach them to the chain—the jump rings and chain are too small to maneuver with your fingers.

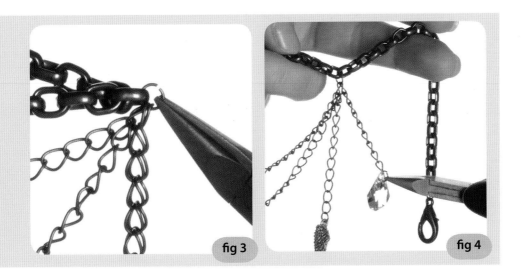

fig 3

fig 4

3: Use 1 jump ring to attach a link of the shorter small chain that is 4¾" (12 cm) from the fold and a link of the longer small chain that is 5½" (14 cm) from the fold to a link of the large chain that is 4¼" (11 cm) from where the last jump ring was attached to it (**figure 3**).

4: Use 1 jump ring to attach the wing charm to the longer of the small-chain ends. Repeat to attach the polygon drop to the shorter small-chain end (**figure 4**). *The jump ring just fits around the polygon drop. It may take a little finessing to close.*

Chain Scale

Sterling silver chain can be very expensive (currently about $13 an ounce), and fine silver chain made by PMC artists can cost even more. But—good news!—not all chain will break the bank. Base metal chain plated with silver, gold, and other metallic finishes is much cheaper than precious metal chain and comes in tons of cool shapes and sizes.

experiment

with sizing

When I first started making jewelry, every necklace I created fell either into the choker (fifteen to sixteen inches) or the princess (eighteen inches) necklace categories—styles I was comfortable wearing.

Now that I have a jewelry box filled with short necklaces, I've finally become bold enough (or should I say bored enough) to experiment with other necklace sizes. Lariats (long, claspless necklaces), I discovered, look great with tops with open necklines, and opera necklaces (twenty-eight inches or longer) can give any outfit a slimmer appearance.

But this chapter isn't just about playing with necklace lengths. It's about playing with earring and bracelet lengths and widths, too. Short-dangle earrings are quick to make and easy to wear but wide chandelier earrings can add more drama to an outfit. Likewise, a lot can be said about one-strand bracelets, but add another strand or two, and I guarantee your wrist will get a little more attention. It all goes to show that size does matter!

Glittery Ears

MATERIALS

6 golden yellow 7x18mm cubic zirconia (CZ) teardrops

2 rhodium-plated 10mm flower charms with indicolite crystals

2 sterling silver 31x43mm corset chandelier earring findings

1 pair of sterling silver 15mm hoop earrings

2 sterling silver 4mm jump rings

18" (45.5 cm) of sterling silver 24-gauge wire

TOOLS

Wire cutters

Flat-nose pliers

Round-nose pliers

FINISHED SIZE

3¼" (8.5 cm)

TECHNIQUES

Wireworking; opening and closing jump rings

etc. . . .

Cubic zirconia beads mimic the weight and clarity of diamonds but cost much less and are available in an array of colors and shapes.

SIMPLICITY SCALE

There's a time and a place for small, dainty earrings. But there's another time and place for big, bold earrings like these, and the huge variety of chandelier findings available makes it easy to create them yourself. I chose to decorate my chandeliers with golden cubic zirconia teardrops and crystal-studded flower charms. I figure my ears deserve to be indulged a little bit now and then.

1: Use 1 jump ring to attach 1 flower charm to the inside loop of 1 earring finding (**figure 1**).

2: String 1 CZ to the center of a 3" (7.5 cm) piece of wire. Bend both ends of the wire up the sides and across the top of the bead. Bend one end of the wire straight up at the center of the bead and wrap the other wire around it to form a few coils (**figure 2**). Form a wrapped loop with the other end of the wire that attaches to one of the bottom loops of the earring finding used in Step 1 and wraps back down over the already-formed coils (**figure 3**). Repeat entire step twice, attaching the CZs to the two remaining earring loops.

3: Open the loop of 1 hoop earring as you would a jump ring. String the top loop of the earring finding, then close the hoop-earring loop.

4: Repeat Steps 1–3 for the other earring.

fig 1   fig 2   fig 3

Emerald Styles

MATERIALS

2 apple green 8mm vintage crystal rounds

2 brass 15.2x21.2mm diamond filigrees

2 brass 9.5mm etched jump rings

2 brass 1" (2.5 cm) 22-gauge eye pins

1 pair of brass 20mm ear wires

TOOLS

Flat-nose pliers

Round-nose pliers

Wire cutters

FINISHED SIZE

2" (5 cm)

TECHNIQUE

Wireworking

SIMPLICITY SCALE

etc. . . .

For a vintage looks that's oh so modern, try filigree findings like the ones used here.

Emerald Styles
go long!

We're always trying to lose the inches, but, in the case of earrings, I recommend you pack them on. Long, delicate earrings add a feminine touch to any outfit and are just as easy to make as short earrings. I promise.

Mine are of medium length and feature vintage apple green crystals that show off nicely against natural brass findings—a look that is retro, yet contemporary. If you're adventurous, take your earrings to even greater lengths by making them long enough to gently sweep your shoulders.

1: Attach the eye end of an eye pin to the top of 1 filigree as you would a jump ring (**figure 1**). String 1 crystal and form a simple loop that attaches to 1 jump ring. Attach the jump ring to 1 ear wire (**figure 2**). Repeat entire step for the other earring.

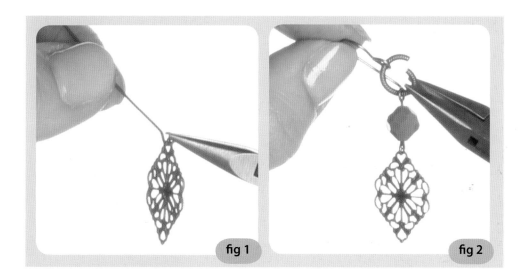

fig 1   fig 2

Royal Arachnid

MATERIALS

50 salmon-lined crystal size 15° seed beads

21 silvery gray 5mm potato pearls

32 silvery gray 8mm potato pearls

1 sterling silver 30x25mm insect box clasp

6 sterling silver 2mm crimp tubes

6 sterling silver 3mm crimp covers

30" (76 cm) of silver-plated .018 beading wire

TOOLS

Wire cutters

Crimping pliers

FINISHED SIZE

7" (18 cm)

TECHNIQUES

Stringing; crimping

etc. . . .

When using a multistrand clasp, make sure the beads of one strand aren't so big as to crowd those of the adjacent strand(s). Doing so will ensure that the piece lies properly on your wrist or neck.

SIMPLICITY SCALE

Multistrand necklaces and bracelets make for eye-catching accessories. My favorite part about designing them is choosing what clasp to use. This project's eccentric clasp features some sort of glamorized creepy crawly. To compliment it, I sandwiched a strand of smaller silver pearls between two strands of larger silver pearls. Isn't it rich?

1: Cut the beading wire into three 10" (25.5 cm) pieces.

2: Use 1 wire to string 1 crimp tube and one loop of one half of the clasp; pass back through the crimp tube and crimp; trim excess wire. Repeat twice to attach the remaining wires to the other two loops of the same half of the clasp. Cover each crimp tube with a crimp cover.

3: Use one of the outside wires to string {one 8mm pearl and 1 seed bead} fifteen times. String one 8mm pearl, 1 crimp tube, and the corresponding outside loop of the other half of the clasp. Pass back through the crimp tube and crimp; trim excess wire and cover tube with a crimp cover. Repeat entire step with the other outside wire.

4: Use the middle wire to string {one 5mm pearl and 1 seed bead} twenty times. String one 5mm pearl, 1 crimp tube, and the middle loop of the other half of the clasp. Pass back through the crimp tube (**figure 1**) and crimp; trim excess wire and cover tube with a crimp cover.

fig 1

Cabling Casablanca

MATERIALS

2 teal and gold 13x22mm vintage
   molded resin ovals

2 vermeil 50mm leaf-end head pins

38" (96.5 cm) of vermeil German metal
   5x8mm oval chain

FINISHED SIZE

41½" (105.5 cm)

TOOLS

Flat-nose pliers

Round-nose pliers

Wire cutters

TECHNIQUE

Wireworking

SIMPLICITY SCALE

Cabling Casablanca

go extra long

Lariats draw attention from the wearer's neck down to her attire. They look especially nice peeking out of an open collar or dripping over the top of a shirt.

Lariats are also very versatile—most can be tied in three ways: folded in half with the loose ends drawn through the loop formed at the fold, both ends used as one to tie an overhand knot, or the ends used separately to tie an overhand knot.

My golden lariat took no time at all to make: I strung the vintage beads onto vermeil leaf-end head pins, which I attached to the ends of the vermeil chain. Talk about easy elegance.

1: Use a head pin to string 1 resin oval and form a wrapped loop that attaches to one end of the chain (**figure 1**). Repeat with the other end of the chain.

fig 1

etc. . . .

Decorative head pins, like the leaf ones used here, can add an extra-special finishing touch to handmade jewelry.

fig 1

fig 2

fig 3

1: Cut the beading wire into eighty-one 4" (10 cm) pieces

2: Use 1 wire to string 45 sapphire seed beads, 1 crimp tube, and the ring of one half of the clasp. Pass back through the tube (**figure 1**) and crimp; trim excess wire.

3: Use 1 wire to string 44 crystal seed beads, 1 crimp tube, and the ring of the same half of the clasp used in Step 2. Pass back through the tube (**figure 2**) and crimp; trim excess wire.

4: Repeat Step 2 with the same half of the clasp. You now have one set of three rings: 1 crystal ring between 2 sapphire rings.

5: Use 1 piece of wire to string 45 sapphire seed beads, 1 crimp tube, and the set of rings formed previously. Pass back through the tube and crimp; trim excess wire.

6: Use 1 piece of wire to string 44 crystal seed beads, 1 crimp tube, and the set of rings formed previously. Pass back through the tube and crimp; trim excess wire.

7: Repeat Step 5 (**figure 3**).

8: Repeat Steps 5–7 twenty-four times, each time connecting a set of 2 sapphire rings and 1 crystal ring to another set of the same.

9: Repeat Steps 2–4 with the other half of the clasp, also connecting the rings to the last set of rings in the chain.

etc. . . .

A special pair of crimping pliers called the Magical Crimp Form Tool turns 2mm crimp tubes used with .014, .015, or .019 beading wire into little silver beads. Used in a project like this, the pliers will help camouflage the crimp tubes.

Mini Must-Haves

Never underestimate the power of the little guys—in this case, seed beads. These tiny, inexpensive rings of glass are available in hundreds of colors and finishes and have many uses in jewelry design. String some into a loop to form a bail or clasp. Use them as spacers between larger beads. Or, make an entire piece of jewelry with them, as in Seeds of Chain.

easy

does it

Handmade jewelry is rewarding to make and fun to wear, but sometimes the time commitment deters even the most creative person. I'm here to tell you that you can make fashionable jewelry fast—like in an hour or less!

String a fun pendant to the center of some leather cord, tie a couple of knots, and, voila, you have a cool new necklace. Slide sequins onto precoiled wire, make loops on the ends that include pretty flower beads, and, voila, you have a beautiful bracelet. Slip a couple of lampworked beads on a pair of earring hoops, and, voila, custom earrings. Get my drift?

In this chapter I'll show you how to create eye-catching projects in three steps or less, thanks, in part, to amazing beading supplies (like rings with loops on top for attaching beads) that make jewelry making a snap. With projects as easy as these, you could whip up a new accessory for every day of the week.

Peace Cord

MATERIALS

1 sterling silver 34mm bird/peace pendant

1 sterling silver 8mm jump ring

28" (71 cm) of black 2mm Greek leather cord

TOOL

Scissors

FINISHED SIZE

16" (40.5 cm), expandable to 24" (61 cm)

TECHNIQUE

Knotting

SIMPLICITY SCALE

etc. . . .

Use real, not imitation, leather
for the best results. Better yet,
use Greek leather cord, a supple,
uniformly colored, high-quality
leather cord, usually made in—
guess where? —Greece!

Peace Cord
knot it

You know how to tie a knot, right? Then you're prepared to make this ridiculously easy necklace that's seriously stylish. Tie two overhand knots to secure the pendant to the center of the cord, then tie two slide knots to create an adjustable neckband. This is a great project for do-it-yourself jewelry makers who want remarkable results right now.

1: Attach the jump ring to the pendant's loop.

2: String the jump ring to the middle of the leather cord. Tie an overhand knot on each side of the jump ring to hold the pendant in place (**figure 1**).

3: To form a slide knot, place one end of the necklace (the working cord) next to the other side of the necklace. Bend the working cord about 3" (7.5 cm) from its end and coil it around the other cord for two or three turns (**figure 2**). Pass the cord end back through the coil created (**figure 3**) and pull tight. Trim tail end. Repeat entire step on the other side of the necklace.

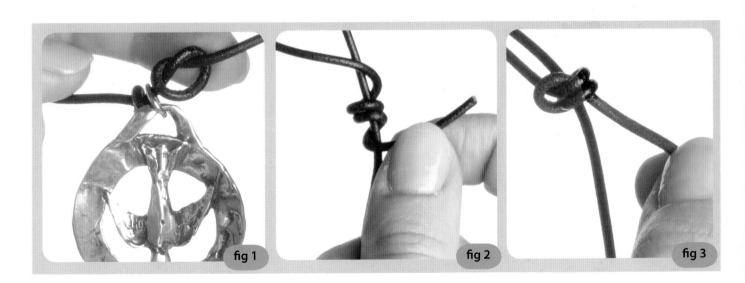

fig 1

fig 2

fig 3

Plastic Posey

MATERIALS

13" (33 cm) of iridescent light brown 8mm flat sequins

3 assorted green Lucite leaves

1 rosaline 22mm vintage Lucite flower

1 smoke topaz matte 36mm vintage Lucite flower

12 Thai silver 4x2mm flower-stamped rondelles

2 sterling silver 6mm jump rings

1 sterling silver 1" (2.5 cm) 22-gauge ball-end head pin

16" (40.5 cm) of stainless steel large-bracelet size memory wire

FINISHED SIZE

14" (35.5 cm)

TOOLS

Memory wire cutters

Flat-nose pliers

Round-nose pliers

TECHNIQUES

Wireworking; stringing; opening and closing jump rings

etc. . . .

This bracelet will be much easier to assemble if you buy sequins on a "worm" (strung on a strand). That way you can string the sequins straight from the strand.

SIMPLICITY SCALE

Plastic Posey

remember memory wire

Memory wire is a hard steel wire that is permanently coiled and hence stays put around your finger, wrist, or neck—sans clasp. One caution: It is so tough it will ruin your wire cutters, so invest in special memory-wire cutters (about $15) or buy a cheap pair of strong pliers from the hardware store.

1: Use the head pin to string 1 rosaline and 1 smoke topaz flower front to back; form a simple loop to create a flower dangle (**figure 1**).

2: Form a simple loop on one end of the memory wire. String {1" (2.5 cm) of sequins and 1 rondelle} twelve times. String 1" (2.5 cm) of sequins, then form a simple loop that attaches to the flower dangle (**figure 2**).

3: Use the jump rings to attach the leaves (2 on one jump ring, 1 on the other) to the first simple loop made (**figure 3**).

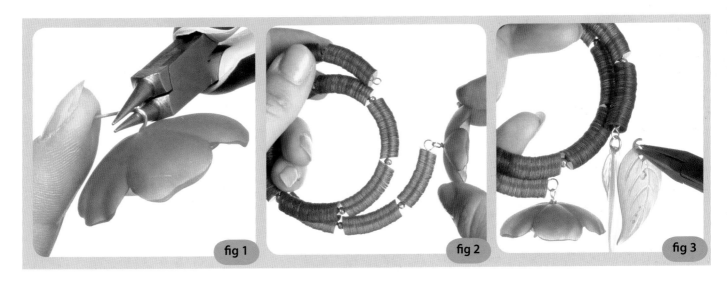

fig 1   fig 2   fig 3

Ring Me

MATERIALS

3 transparent garnet 2x5mm pressed-glass
   rondelles

6 opaque green 3x6mm pressed-glass
   rondelles

3 yellow 6x5mm pressed-glass flowers

12 sterling silver 1½" (3.8 cm) 24-gauge ball-
   end head pins

1 Thai silver embellishment ring

TOOLS

Flat-nose pliers

Round-nose pliers

Wire cutters

TECHNIQUE

Wireworking

FINISHED SIZE

Your ring size

SIMPLICITY SCALE

This ring is a great example of a piece of jewelry made using an ingenious, designer-friendly finding: a ring with a loop on top just waiting to be embellished. Many manufacturers offer similar rings, and they're usually available in the most common ring sizes.

Though making this project is not hard (you simply string beads on head pins and attach them to the ring loop using wirewrapped loops), the more crowded the ring loop gets with dangles, the harder it is to add more. And you do want to add more—this ring looks best when it's bursting with beads!

1: Use a head pin to string 1 garnet rondelle. Repeat to string 1 of the remaining beads on each head pin.

2: Form wrapped loops to attach the head pins to the loop of the ring (**figure 1**) in the following order: 1 garnet, 1 green, 1 garnet, 1 green, 1 yellow, 1 green, 1 yellow, 1 green, 1 yellow, 2 green, and 1 garnet.

3: *Variation*: To make the blue ring, use 6 blue 4x6mm button pearls and 6 milky iridescent white 6x5mm pressed-glass flowers.

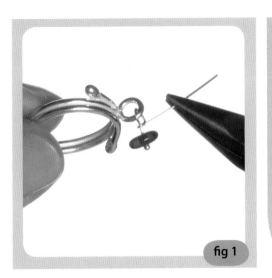

fig 1

etc. . . .

Use longer-than-necessary head pins (more leverage for wrapping the beads) and pliers with long, tapered noses (such as round-nose or needle-nose pliers) to get into the tight spaces you'll encounter in this project.

resources

MATERIALS:

FIND YOUR INSPIRATION

Golden Everglades p. 26
Crystals: Beyond Beadery
Ring connectors and clasp: Pacific Silverworks
Chain and wire: Beading House
Rhinestone Garden p. 30
Crystals: Beyond Beadery
Pendant: Jennifer Morris Beads
Clasp: Nina Designs
Chain: Wynwoods Gallery & Bead Studio
Wire: FusionBeads.com
Leopards and Limes p. 34
Seed beads: Beyond Beadery
Silver rondelles, clasp, head pins, and chain: The Whole Bead Shop
Similar lampworked rondelles: Michele Goldstein
Back in Black p. 38
All materials: FusionBeads.com
Little Devil p. 40
Glass rectangles: Raven's Journey International
Word beads: Ornamentea
Fine silver pendant, clasp, and chain: Zoa Art
Leather cord: Shipwreck Beads
Family Style p. 44
Crystals: Beyond Beadery
Pearls: PearlBeadSale.com
Fine silver charms: Kate McKinnon
Bezel links: Susan Lenart Kazmer
Clasp: Pacific Silverwork
Jump rings: Via Murano
Head pins: Fire Mountain Gems and Beads
Amazing Glaze: Ornamentea
Glue: Michaels

MIX IT UP

Punchy & Dotty p. 50
Lucite beads and 13mm chain: The Beadin' Path
Lampworked beads: Sarah Moran
17x7mm chain: Metalliferous
Jump rings: Fire Mountain Gems and Beads
Snap Fizz Pop p. 54
Glass rondelles: Raven's Journey International
Bottle cap beads: Glass Garden Beads
Snowflake spacers: Kamol (wholesale only)
Toggle clasp: Saki Silver
Crimp tubes and covers: FusionBeads.com
Beading wire: Beadalon (wholesale only)
Twiggy p. 56
Turquoise and wire: Fire Mountain Gems and Beads
Pewter birdies, copper chain, and jump ring mélange: Ornamentea
Pine cone charm and flat cable chain: FusionBeads.com
Leaf charm: Nina Designs
Twig pendants: Scattered Light Jewelry
Clasp: Springall Adventures
Brass chain: Rishashay
Gold chain: The Whole Bead Shop
Leaf connectors and tree pendant: Green Girl Studios

Big Sky Bling p. 60
Clay rondelles: Xaz Bead Company
8mm spacers: Somerset Silver (wholesale only)
Daisy spacers: Singaraja Imports
Thai silver barrels: Multi Creations
Bumpy barrels and button: Springall Adventures
Leather: Shipwreck Beads
Posh Porcupine p. 62
Lampworked beads: MoonBeads Glass Art
Clasp: HandFast
Crimp tubes and covers: FusionBeads.com
Beading wire: Beadalon (wholesale only)
Not for Wallflowers p. 66
Lucite: The Beadin' Path
Clasps: Fire Mountain Gems and Beads
Silk ribbon: Silk Painting is Fun

PLAY WITH SYMMETRY

Brass Menagerie p. 70
Pressed-glass flowers: Raven's Journey International
Brass beads and findings: Vintaj Natural Brass Co. (wholesale only)
Aqua Bloom p. 76
Seed beads: Beyond Beadery
Apetite: Artgems Inc.
Citrine: Papio Creek Gems & Gifts
Fire-polished beads: Raven's Journey International
Thai silver rondelles: Somerset Silver (wholesale only)
Pewter link and charm: Green Girl Studios
Lampworked flower pendant: Gail Crosman Moore
Crimp tubes and covers: FusionBeads.com
Beading wire: Beadalon (wholesale only)
All Abuzz p. 80
Moonstone: Artgems Inc.
Onyx bead: Lumina Inspirations
Bee clasp: Green Girl Studios
Bee charm: Candice Wakumoto
Sterling silver round: Saki Silver
CZs, crimp tubes, and covers: Fusionbeads.com
Beading wire: Beadalon (wholesale only)
Jump ring: Via Murano
Sorbet Songbird p. 82
Seed beads: Beyond Beadery
Dagger beads: Bokamo Designs
Lampworked discs: Blue Heeler Glass
Moonstone and opal: Artgems Inc.
Thai silver tubes: Saki Silver
Clasp: Green Girl Studios
Jump rings: FusionBeads.com
Industrial Chic p. 86
Fine silver charms: Wynwoods Gallery & Bead Studio
Jump ring: Via Murano
Ear wires: FusionBeads.com
Dark Angel p. 88
Crystal drop: FusionBeads.com
Wing charm: Shipwreck Beads
Oxidized chain, jump rings, and clasp: The Whole Bead Shop

EXPERIMENT WITH SIZING

Glittery Ears p. 94
All materials: FusionBeads.com
Emerald Styles p. 96
Crystals: Beyond Beadery
Brass findings: Vintaj Natural Brass Co. (wholesale only)
Royal Arachnid p. 98
Clasp: Jess Imports (wholesale only)
8mm pearls: Austin Gem & Bead
5mm pearls: JP Jewelry and Co.
Seed beads: Beyond Beadery
Cabling Casablanca p. 100
Resin ovals: Earthly Adornments
Head pins: Shiana
Chain: The Whole Bead Shop
Seeds of Chain p. 102
Seed beads: Beyond Beadery
Clasp: Kamol (wholesale only)
Crimp tubes: Fire Mountain Gems and Beads

EASY DOES IT

Peace Cord p. 108
Leather cord: Shipwreck Beads
Dove/peace pendant: Springall Adventures
Jump rings: Via Murano
Hoop Hoop Hooray p. 110
Lampworked discs: Kennebunkport Bead Art
Hoop earrings: The Whole Bead Shop
Plastic Posey p. 112
Sequins: Beads and Beyond or General Bead
Lucite leaves and flowers: Echo Artworks or The Beadin' Path
Jump rings: Via Murano
A Toggle to Ogle p. 114
Clasp: Zoa Art. Jump rings: Via Murano
Chain: Kamol (wholesale only)
Ring Me p. 116
Garnet rondelles and yellow flower beads: Raven's Journey International
Opaque green rondelles: Via Murano
Head pins: Fire Mountain Gems and Beads
Ring: Somerset Silver (wholesale only)

SOURCES:

Artgems Inc.
Gemstones, semiprecious stones, and more
4860 E. Baseline Rd., Mesa, AZ 85206
(480) 545-6009
www.artgemsinc.com

Austin Gem & Bead
Pearls, gemstones, and more
PO Box 719, Chestertown, MD 21620
info@beadivine.com
www.austingemandbead.com

Beadalon (wholesale only)
All beading supplies
440 Highlands Blvd., Coatesville, PA 19320
(866) 423-2325
www.beadalon.com

Beadin' Path, The
Vintage Lucite, Swarovski crystals, and more
15 Main St., Freeport, ME 04032
(877) 92-BEADS
www.beadinpath.com

Beading House
Metal beads and chain
14510 NE 20th St., Ste. 104B
Bellevue, WA 98007
(877) 496-8663
www.beadinghouse.com

Beads and Beyond
All beading supplies
25 102nd Ave. NE, Bellevue, WA 98004
(425) 462-8992

Beyond Beadery
Seed beads and Swarovski crystals
PO Box 460, Rollinsville, CO 80474
(800) 840-5548
www.beyondbeadery.com

Blue Heeler Glass
Lampworked beads
Box 118, Lyman, NE 69352
(308) 787-9999
www.blueheelerglass.com

Bokomo Designs
Czech glass and lampworked beads
5609 W. 99th St., Overland Park, KS 66207
(913) 648-4296
www.bokomodesigns.com

Candice Wakumoto
Fine silver beads and findings
PO Box 893113, Mililani, HI 96789
(808) 625-2706
candicewakumoto@msn.com